SECOND EDITION

SATB SAX QUARTET
Score and Parts
-Soprano Sax
-Alto Sax
-Tenor Sax
-Bari Sax

I0620372

10 Christmas Songs FOR SATB Sax Quartet

Jeff Bratz

Sign up for the HarmonyTabs email list to keep up with new music releases, upcoming publications, and promotions:

HARMONYTABS EMAIL LIST

10 CHRISTMAS SONGS FOR SATB SAX QUARTET
SECOND EDITION
Copyright © 2025 Jeff Bratz

To request permission, contact the publisher at publishing@HarmonyTabsMusic.com

ISBN: 978-1-961735-18-7 (paperback)
ISBN: 978-1-961735-19-4 (eBook)
ISMN: 979-0-60026-062-1 (paperback)
ISMN: 979-0-60026-063-8 (eBook)

First paperback edition October 2022

Printed in the United States of America

HarmonyTabs Music

HarmonyTabsMusic.com

Contents

INTRO

First, thank you for buying this songbook. I know there are a lot of options out there and I'm honored you landed here.

I hope these songs will be as fun for you to play through as they were for me to arrange. I've always loved the holiday season and I think that's largely due to the music that fills the air in every store, car, home, and everywhere else. I like to believe that in some small part this book will add to the spirit.

On the last page of the score and on each part is a QR code. That code will lead you to a homepage for that song where you can find additional resources including audio/video where you can hear the tune and find optional rehearsal tracks.

If at any point you have any questions, comments, suggestions, or anything else, please feel free to drop me a line: Jeff@HarmonyTabs.com.

Happy music-ing!
-Jeff

ANGELS WE HAVE HEARD ON HIGH

Traditional French Carol
Arr. Jeff Bratz

AWHHOH (SaxQ)
11-11-2024

ANGELS WE HAVE HEARD ON HIGH

AWHHOH (SaxQ)
11-11-2024

ANGELS WE HAVE HEARD ON HIGH

Soprano Saxophone

Traditional French Carol
Arr. Jeff Bratz

AWHHOH (SaxQ)
11-11-2024

Additional resources for this arrangement

ANGELS WE HAVE HEARD ON HIGH

Alto Saxophone

Traditional French Carol
Arr. Jeff Bratz

Additional resources for this arrangement

AWHHOH (SaxQ)
11-11-2024

- 5 -

ANGELS WE HAVE HEARD ON HIGH

Tenor Saxophone

Traditional French Carol
Arr. Jeff Bratz

AWHHOH (SaxQ)
11-11-2024

- 6 -

Additional resources for this arrangement

ANGELS WE HAVE HEARD ON HIGH

Baritone Saxophone

Traditional French Carol
Arr. Jeff Bratz

Additional resources for this arrangement

AWHHOH (SaxQ)
11-11-2024

AULD LANG SYNE

Poem by Robert Burns
Arr. Jeff Bratz

ALS (SQ)
11-11-24

ISMN: 979-0-60026-065-2

- 8 -

AULD LANG SYNE

ALS (SQ)
11-11-24

AULD LANG SYNE

Poem by Robert Burns
Arr. Jeff Bratz

ALS (SQ)
11-11-24

Additional
resources for
this arrangement

AULD LANG SYNE

Alto Saxophone

Poem by Robert Burns
Arr. Jeff Bratz

Additional resources for this arrangement

ALS (SQ)
11-11-24

Tenor Saxophone

AULD LANG SYNE

Poem by Robert Burns
Arr. Jeff Bratz

AULD LANG SYNE

Baritone Saxophone

Poem by Robert Burns
Arr. Jeff Bratz

Additional resources for this arrangement

ALS (SQ)
11-11-24

AWAY IN A MANGER

William J. Kirkpatrick
and James R. Murray
Arr. Jeff Bratz

AIAM (SaxQ)
11-14-24

AWAY IN A MANGER

AIAM (SaxQ)
11-14-24

AWAY IN A MANGER

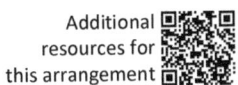
AIAM (SaxQ)
11-14-24

AWAY IN A MANGER

Soprano Saxophone

William J. Kirkpatrick
and James R. Murray
Arr. Jeff Bratz

AIAM (SaxQ)
11-14-24

Additional resources for this arrangement

AWAY IN A MANGER

Alto Saxophone

William J. Kirkpatrick
and James R. Murray
Arr. Jeff Bratz

All Rights Reserved
©2019 HarmonyTabs Music
www.HarmonyTabsMusic.com
ISMN: 979-0-60026-066-9

- 19 -

AIAM (SaxQ)
11-14-24

AIAM (SaxQ)
11-14-24

Additional resources for this arrangement

AWAY IN A MANGER

Baritone Saxophone

William J. Kirkpatrick
and James R. Murray
Arr. Jeff Bratz

AIAM (SaxQ)
11-14-24

DECK THE HALLS

Traditional Welsh Carol
Arr. Jeff Bratz

DTH (SaxQ)
11-18-24

DECK THE HALLS

DTH (SaxQ)
11-18-24

DECK THE HALLS

DECK THE HALLS

DTH (SaxQ)
11-18-24

DECK THE HALLS

DTH (SaxQ)
11-18-24

DECK THE HALLS

Soprano Saxophone

Traditional Welsh Carol
Arr. Jeff Bratz

DTH (SaxQ)
11-18-24

DECK THE HALLS

Alto Saxophone

Traditional Welsh Carol
Arr. Jeff Bratz

DTH (SaxQ)
11-18-24

DTH (SaxQ)
11-18-24

DECK THE HALLS

Tenor Saxophone

Traditional Welsh Carol
Arr. Jeff Bratz

DTH (SaxQ)
11-18-24

DECK THE HALLS

DTH (SaxQ)
11-18-24

DTH (SaxQ)
11-18-24

THE FIRST NOEL

Traditional English Carol
Arr. Jeff Bratz

TFN (SAXQ)
11-19-24

TFN (SAXQ)
11-19-24

THE FIRST NOEL

TFN (SAXQ)
11-19-24

THE FIRST NOEL

TFN (SAXQ)
11-19-24

THE FIRST NOEL

Soprano Saxophone

Traditional English Carol
Arr. Jeff Bratz

Additional resources for this arrangement

TFN (SAXQ)
11-19-24

Alto Saxophone

THE FIRST NOEL

Traditional English Carol
Arr. Jeff Bratz

TFN (SAX@)
11-19-24

Additional
resources for
this arrangement

THE FIRST NOEL

Tenor Saxophone

Traditional English Carol
Arr. Jeff Bratz

Additional resources for this arrangement

TFN (SAXQ)
11-19-24

THE FIRST NOEL

Baritone Saxophone

Traditional English Carol
Arr. Jeff Bratz

TFN (SAXQ)
11-19-24

Additional resources for this arrangement

GO TELL IT ON THE MOUNTAIN

COMPILED BY
JOHN WESLEY WORK, JR.
ARR. JEFF BRATZ

GT1OTM (SaxQ)
11-21-24

GO TELL IT ON THE MOUNTAIN

GO TELL IT ON THE MOUNTAIN

GT1DTM (SaxQ)
11-21-24

GO TELL IT ON THE MOUNTAIN

Soprano Saxophone

Compiled by
John Wesley Work, Jr.
Arr. Jeff Bratz

Additional resources for this arrangement

GT1OTM (SaxQ)
11-21-24

GO TELL IT ON THE MOUNTAIN

Alto Saxophone

Compiled by
John Wesley Work, Jr.
Arr. Jeff Bratz

GTIOTM (SaxQ)
11-21-24
ISMN: 979-0-60026-068-3

- 48 -

Additional resources for this arrangement

GO TELL IT ON THE MOUNTAIN

Tenor Saxophone

Compiled by
John Wesley Work, Jr.
Arr. Jeff Bratz

GT1OTM (SaxQ)
11-21-24

GO TELL IT ON THE MOUNTAIN

Baritone Saxophone

Compiled by
John Wesley Work, Jr.
Arr. Jeff Bratz

GT1OTM (SaxQ)
11-21-24

Additional resources for this arrangement

GOD REST YE MERRY, GENTLEMEN

19th Century English Carol
Arr. Jeff Bratz

GRYMG (SaxQ)
11-22-24

GOD REST YE MERRY, GENTLEMEN

GOD REST YE MERRY, GENTLEMEN

GRYMG (SaxQ)
11-22-24

GOD REST YE MERRY, GENTLEMEN

GOD REST YE MERRY, GENTLEMEN

Soprano Saxophone

19th Century English Carol
Arr. Jeff Bratz

GRYMG (SaxQ)
11-22-24

God Rest Ye Merry, Gentlemen

GRYMG (SaxQ)
11-22-24

GOD REST YE MERRY, GENTLEMEN

Alto Saxophone

19th Century English Carol
Arr. Jeff Bratz

GRYMG (SaxQ)
11-22-24

GOD REST YE MERRY, GENTLEMEN

GOD REST YE MERRY, GENTLEMEN

Tenor Saxophone

19th Century English Carol
Arr. Jeff Bratz

GRYMG (SaxQ)
11-22-24

GOD REST YE MERRY, GENTLEMEN

GRYMG (SaxQ)
11-22-24

GOD REST YE MERRY, GENTLEMEN

Baritone Saxophone

19th Century English Carol
Arr. Jeff Bratz

GRYMG (SaxQ)
11-22-24

GOD REST YE MERRY, GENTLEMEN

HALLELUJAH CHORUS
(ABRIDGED)

George Friedrich Handel
Arr. Jeff Bratz

HC (SaxQ)
11-26-24

HALLELUJAH CHORUS (ABRIDGED)

HC (SaxQ)
11-26-24

HC (SaxQ)
11-26-24

HALLELUJAH CHORUS (ABRIDGED)

HC (SaxQ)
11-26-24

HALLELUJAH CHORUS
(ABRIDGED)

Soprano Saxophone

George Friedrich Handel
Arr. Jeff Bratz

Additional resources for this arrangement

HC (SaxQ)
11-26-24

Alto Saxophone

HALLELUJAH CHORUS
(ABRIDGED)

George Friedrich Handel
Arr. Jeff Bratz

HC (SaxQ)
11-26-24

- 68 -

Additional
resources for
this arrangement

HALLELUJAH CHORUS
(ABRIDGED)

Tenor Saxophone

George Friedrich Handel
Arr. Jeff Bratz

Additional resources for this arrangement

HC (SaxQ)
11-26-24

Baritone Saxophone

HALLELUJAH CHORUS
(ABRIDGED)

George Friedrich Handel
Arr. Jeff Bratz

HC (SaxQ)
11-26-24

Additional resources for this arrangement

HARK! THE HERALD ANGELS SING

Felix Mendelssohn
Lyrics by Charles Wesley
and George Whitefield
Arr. Jeff Bratz

HTHAS (SaxQ)
12-10-24

HARK! THE HERALD ANGELS SING

HTHAS (SaxQ)
12-10-24

HARK! THE HERALD ANGELS SING

HTHAS (SaxQ)
12-10-24

HTHAS (SaxQ)
12-10-24

Additional
resources for
this arrangement

HARK! THE HERALD ANGELS SING

Soprano Saxophone

Felix Mendelssohn
Lyrics by Charles Wesley
and George Whitefield
Arr. Jeff Bratz

HTHAS (SaxQ)
12-10-24

HARK! THE HERALD ANGELS SING

Alto Saxophone

Felix Mendelssohn
Lyrics by Charles Wesley
and George Whitefield
Arr. Jeff Bratz

HTHAS (SaxQ)
12-10-24

Additional resources for this arrangement

HARK! THE HERALD ANGELS SING

Tenor Saxophone

Felix Mendelssohn
Lyrics by Charles Wesley
and George Whitefield
Arr. Jeff Bratz

Additional resources for this arrangement

HTHAS (SaxQ)
12-10-24

HARK! THE HERALD ANGELS SING

Baritone Saxophone

Felix Mendelssohn
Lyrics by Charles Wesley
and George Whitefield
Arr. Jeff Bratz

HTHAS (SaxQ)
12-10-24

Additional resources for this arrangement

I SAW THREE SHIPS

Traditional
Arr. Jeff Bratz

ISTS (SaxQ)
12-16-24

I SAW THREE SHIPS

I SAW THREE SHIPS

ISTS (SaxQ)
12-16-24

ISTS (SaxQ)
12-16-24

I SAW THREE SHIPS

ISTS (SaxQ)
12-16-24

I SAW THREE SHIPS

Soprano Saxophone

Traditional
Arr. Jeff Bratz

Soprano Saxophone
I SAW THREE SHIPS

ISTS (SaxQ)
12-16-24

I SAW THREE SHIPS

Alto Saxophone

Traditional
Arr. Jeff Bratz

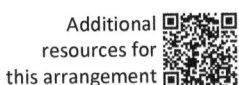
ISTS (SaxQ)
12-16-24

Tenor Saxophone

I SAW THREE SHIPS

Traditional
Arr. Jeff Bratz

ISTS (SaxQ)
12-16-24

I SAW THREE SHIPS

ISTS (SaxQ)
12-16-24

I SAW THREE SHIPS

Baritone Saxophone

Traditional
Arr. Jeff Bratz

I SAW THREE SHIPS

 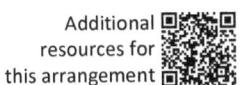

ISTS (SaxQ)
12-16-24

FINAL WORDS

Please consider leaving a review of this book. I would greatly appreciate it. It will help me to continue on this book writing journey I've set off on.

Thank you in advance!

Leave a Review

HARMONYTABS EMAIL LIST

Once again, here is the link to the HarmonyTabs email list to keep you up to speed on any new music, publications, and promotions.

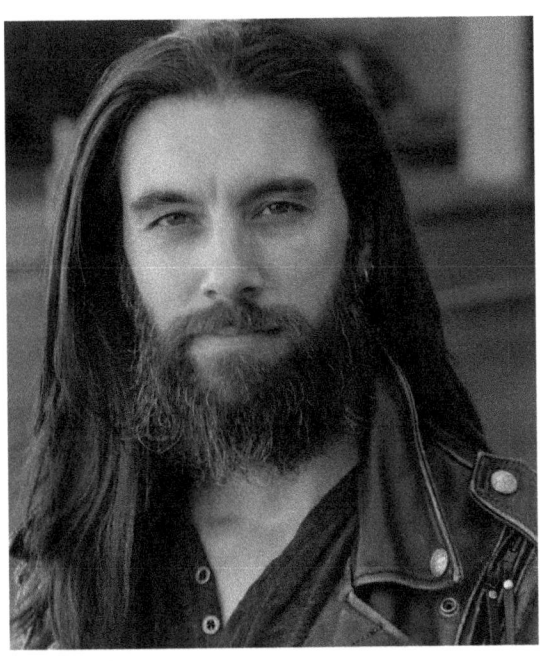

ABOUT THE AUTHOR

Jeff Bratz has a degree in Professional Music from the School for Music Vocations and a Professional Certificate in Music Theory and Composition from Berklee College of Music. He's a composer and arranger specializing in vocal arrangements. In a former life, Jeff was a music teacher for grades pre-k through high school. He has sung in dozens of vocal groups including The Dickens Carolers at Disneyland's *Club 33*, The Fault Line on *America's Got Talent*, and Manhattan Transfer tribute group LA Transfer. He was also part of the Downbeat award-winning First Take. He currently performs with rock band RaDIUM, 80s rock tribute band 8IGHTY 6IXX, and salsa band Calle Mambo. He lives in Pasadena with his wonderful partner Kristen and the cutest nugget that ever nuggeted: Ollie!

Also Available From

HarmonyTabs

Sheet Music

-A Cappella Choirs/Groups
-Brass Ensembles
-String Ensembles
-Sax Ensembles
And More!

HARMONYTABS.COM/SHEET-MUSIC/

Songbooks

-Wind Ensembles
-A Cappella Choirs/Groups
-Flute Ensembles
-Brass Ensembles
And More!

HARMONYTABS.COM/MUSIC-BOOKS/SONGBOOKS/

Music Theory and Instruction

-An Incomplete Crash Course
in Contemporary Music Theory:
The Fundamentals

More to Come!

HARMONYTABS.COM/MUSIC-BOOKS/INSTRUCTIONAL-BOOKS/

Music Composition

-Standard Manuscript Notebook
-Pocket Manuscript Notebook
-Writing Prompt Journals

More to Come!

HARMONYTABS.COM/MUSIC-BOOKS/MUSIC-COMPOSITION-BOOKS/

HarmonyTabsMusic.com